# GOMORRAH

# GOMORRAH

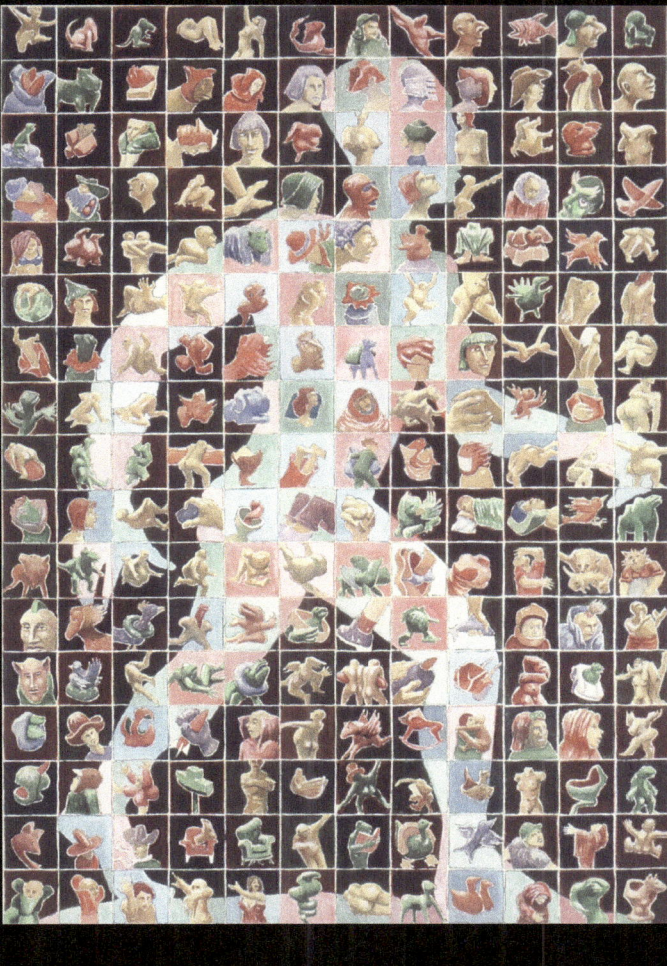

## PICTURES: Richard Wilson
## WORDS: Kenneth Rosen

Poems copyright © 2017 Kenneth Rosen
Paintings copyright © 2017 Richard Wilson

ISBN-13: 978-1-942515-91-3

Photograph of Richard Wilson by Diane Hudson.
Photograph of Kenneth Rosen by Patty Rosen.

Fomite
58 Peru Street
Burlington, VT 05401
www.fomitepress.com

—at the least, a phrase, that phrase,
A hawk of life, that latined phrase:

To know; a missal for brooding sight.
To meet that hawk's eye and to flinch

Not at the eye but at the joy of it.
I play. But this is what I think.

WALLACE STEVENS

1. Prairie Dog & Kite

2. Sunset in the Tunnel

3. Niagara

4. The River

5. Confessional

6. The Mountain

# 1. Prairie Dog & Kite

Landed in the garden of Gomorrah
And squatted, the flag of a flying saucer,
Translucent as a jellyfish, with poison whips!
(He couldn't picture her anymore,
Nor touch!  But they went on
Talking, touching, one night
On gravel and pine needles

Like amorous salmon who'd
Eluded the opaque transparencies
Weird music queered the air, and an amazing
Sky! All of starlight's sweet and scary thrill
Erased by the dull ache of memory!)
A prairie dog rising

To stand, stare and survey, couldn't tell
If his pasture were covered with grass
Or sand, ash or snow!
Except for a familiar hole and a cold burrow,
To do but watch while his old
Red and white kite discovered

It didn't need the tether
That once tugged it aloft!  Since the string
Was so useless and frayed, he tried to drop it,
Being a dog in the dark, let the son-of-a-bitch
Kite hit a wire or cloud!  Or go to hell
For love of flight and lies of fire, and hope
It consumed them!

## 2. Sunset in the Tunnel

There were hooks we never saw
Or clearly understood
On the bottoms of our boats,
Our little dinghies, those dwarf gondolas!
I hated their plastic seat cushions
And cutesy names like First Crush!
Blind Passion! and True Love!

(Yet isn't it always one of the above!?)
I loved it when we groped each other's
Nethers at the bottom of the boat!
What I loved less was the muddy darkness
And stench of watery decrepitude
Which gripped us with foreknowledge

And hoarse cornets which cropped up
And poured forth from half-
Concealed and tinny little speakers!
But the hooks! Those occult hooks
Tied us to a chain on a wheel
That impelled us forward
Bumping along odd docks

Or the tunnel walls, so that ideally
We'd put our arms around each other,
And unload on each other emotionally!
Then fortune (that chain!) released us
Into illusory eddies where some
Jack-in-the-box or garish hag
Would jump up, "Ha! Ha! Ha!"

Enough rough noise
And abrupt light to startle
Us lovers, us fools on our relentlessly
Cheap trip to crash against each other's hearts!
I felt yours! And that was the easy part, and
Fun! But the light at the end of the tunnel
Was sunset, a rainbow of basic purple,

Blood red and black, slowly
Shifting above a miniature
Frayed papier maché Grand Canyon,
Coated with painted sand
And glue, because it was End-
of-the-Ride, sweetie, and time,
According to everything, to whisper
Goodbye, and kiss! I couldn't

Face it, though I knew I had to!
Which is why in order to act brave
I brought you this bouquet of blue lilies,
Moments of light, and dark roses!

## 3. Niagara

He said he loved her!
Which eventuated in his attempting Niagara Fal[ls]
In a wheelbarrow!  Someone let loose
Of its handles!  Her!  La belle dame sans
Merci!  But what use
Was a Thank you!? Christ, he had lots of time
To think!  Would this look better

From Canada?!  Did resisting his severe desire
To seize a mossy rock or flimsy
Branch improve his chances?  At what?
Life after Niagara?  The toothbrush
Armpits he loved to snuffle and suck?
Or their idea!  Later he remembered
A rainbow, an apocalyptic roar

A crash! Something
Must have hit her, made her let go
As if a burn victim nobody could touch
Anymore! Especially him! Did he
Even know her? How stupid to be afloat
On the upper Niagara
In a wheelbarrow, thinking all was

Safe as the Queen Elizabeth!  Its naked
Handles, its rudder!  Say goodbye,
Failed sailor!  You and your tainted paper!
Tainted canvas!  Tainted skin!
There is nowhere after Niagara
But death and the future!  And
Nothing for you here!

# 4. The River

As for that ache, lover, aspirin
Could ease it along awhile,
Or prayer, for another twenty-four hours,
Month or year, so we can see what we've got:
Romance? Modus vivendi? Or a bad slide
Down an average mountain, stumps,
Outcropped rocks and ravines
Visited inevitably by life's lubricities!

Stop worrying like a child
Who can't control its hands, or a dog
Snuffling its balls to see if they're still there
After you've kicked it, so tired
Of its lamentable, almost vulgar
Valentine becoming a flounder!
Misery is so cross-eyed,
And such a bottom feeder! Meanwhile

There's love-life, a river
Loaded with dead bodies not merely
Afloat but catapulting forward
In its tirelessly fresh,
Unhesitant momentum, some spurred
Into impromptu handsprings or almost comic
Jesus imitations, sprung upright,
Skating forward as if alive!
Others, hung up on log or rock

Provoke spectacular geysers,
Even jams of arms and legs, but these
Are temporary! It's funny, even queerly
Reassuring to see their bodies
Come unglued and go flying
With everyone else's into oblivion! Yet of all
Places, it is here we've come,
Ourselves half-dead, to build
A bridge so we won't get wet

Swept up, swept asunder and all that!
But my God, why don't we just
Go back where we came from,
Where we don't need bridges and the air
And our faces are quiet and still unsprayed
By the waters of death, our eyes
Unscarred by figures of terror
That are merely of nakedness:

Tits and hair, dongs, the crack
Of an ass! Winter is coming,
And although the river never freezes
Or lacks its full complement
Of dead bodies of every gender and preference,
How long can we live on bare ground
Or mud, in a tent of bloody skin
Stripped from those with a more genuine

Aptitude for wildness!  So unlike our own,
Timid, inconsistent, requiring promises
Or a plan!  Truth is, we don't
Stay anywhere for long,

But wander back and forth, from safe village
To dangerous river, until we too
Are baffled numb, deprived
Of memory, caution, and clothing,
And swept away!

5. Confessional

## 1. What I Looked For, What I Found

When I looked for a rock I found water,
Filthy, brackish water! It was frozen,
I thought I could tell this was from the trash
Stuck in it, but when I tried to walk across it

On a wide swath of lip, pale mortar
Which stretched behind me forever,
And because I couldn't cry out anywhere,
Having lost my right to a voice in all this,
I tried to save myself and float like the rock

By the idea of a dear-God-save-me prayer!
And also I tried to hide the dirty ice-water
Frozen inside me, the awful wall with stupidly cruel
Grimacing shards of glass someone full of
Blind pride and anger, really

## 2. What Man Makes

Father-force-of-the-sun,
Who made me out of slime
And never let me forget it,
And bade me crawl and stand straight

Until Brother-hunger-for-love bent
And cleft me with his double-headed ax
(Optional horns of every truth!)
That never had to touch me,

As if all of how were: Don't explain,
Don't complain! Just make something
Out of your dirt, and after that

Make something out of what you make,
O-powerless-little-love-and-hate!

## 3. What I Left Out

I keep thinking I've left something out,
How any day I'd find that shy flower of someone's voice
Hiding somewhere, waiting for me to pluck it,
How then its echo, which had been hiding inside me,
A little hope, would begin to prance again
Like a hero, and all the cares of my life

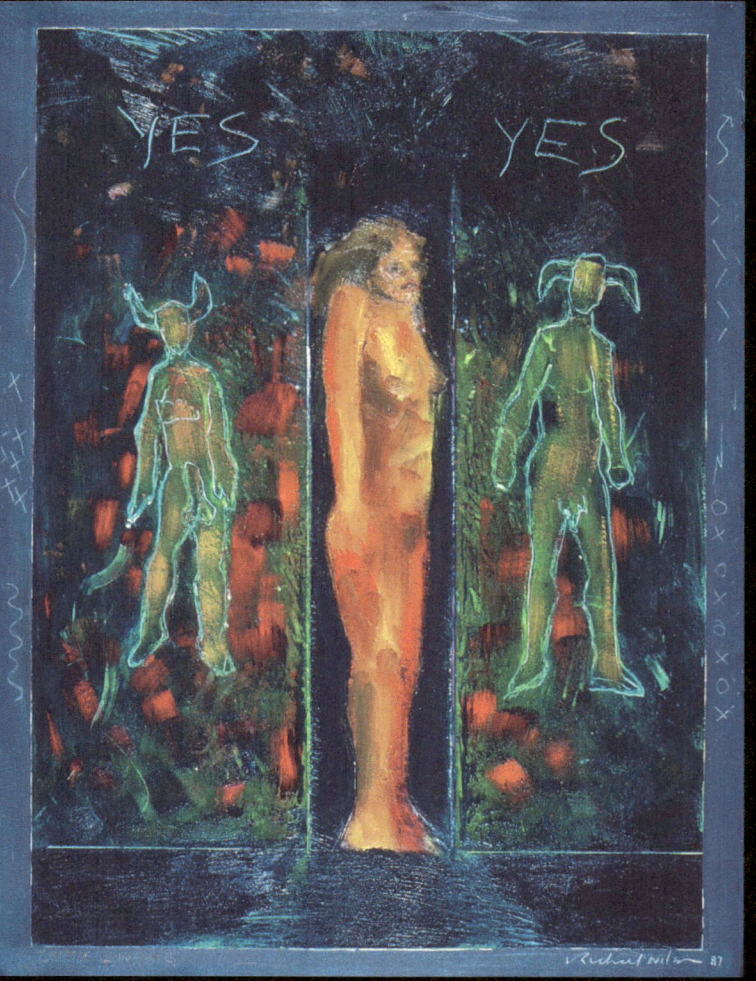

Would grow small or light until sometime late
In the day I would see someone's absolutely uncanny
Face and all cares would vanish, vanish away.
I think I left something out, because today
This hint of violins and wisp of bells' sweetness
Is absent, and nothing makes me prance or swagger,

Absence is my shadow, my companion, being something
Left out, nowhere, not together, not alone!

# 6. The Mountain

There was no way out of Gomorrah
Except through colored lights
They had strung around the border!
So after the year-long roller coaster,
Where I cried out like Tarzan ascending,
Crossing my fingers, closing my eyes
Tight going down, whispering
No interior snapshots, no conversations
And no reverie, ground fog
Insufficiently obscuring litter of

Come—O—Jesus kleenex, headless Venus
Baring her breasts and chestnut
Brush in her kitchen window, ruined grass
Where people relieved themselves,
Had sex or whisky—*the night
I gave you the rose quartz and the fire
In you was the fire in me*—I staggered
Smack into a ferris wheel, a vertical circle
Instead of horizontal, but still a circle,

Slow but high, but I was sick
Of vertigo as either a callisthenic
Or commodity, so one Sunday
I left my funhouse home of twisted mirrors
And black tunnels and drove west
To the White Mountains of love and death
And the wilderness which is like Judah
And where the Psalmist was forever either
Wild or bewildered, which mean the same
Yet are different as awful and awesome,

Climbed a blindfolded face of granite
Justice—(actually, East Royce)—and achieved
The summit at no sunset, gray clouds
Having rolled over New Hampshire, though
Sunlight somehow dappled western Maine,
Kezar Lake, forests, fields and mountains,
And since I was alone (I'd skipped my sandwich
And eaten my navel orange), I let myself
Brood in easy elation how climbing up and down
That mile and a half of birch and fir

Gave me myself as Good dog—*Good dog!*—
So when Rover got back to his nightblue truck,
He drove to a picnic table overlooking the Mahoosics
And polished off his smoked turkey sandwich
With a split of red wine! Thought
Is a tonic! Don't forget it! Get out
To the mountain and do it again sometime!
Think like a dog! All may yet be fine!

Richard Wilson has shown his paintings around the United States and maintains a studio in Portland, Maine.

Kenneth Rosen lives in Portland, Maine. He has published ten collections of poems, most recently, during a Fulbright (2005-06) in Cyprus, Homo Politico, and the duel volume, Cyprus's Bad Period, with The Passport You Ask For, by Turkish-American poet, Adnan Adam Onart.

## About Fomite

*A fomite is a medium capable of transmitting infectious organisms from one individual to another.*

"The activity of art is based on the capacity of people to be infected by the feelings of others." Tolstoy, *What Is Art?*

Writing a review on Amazon, Good Reads, Shelfari, Library Thing or other social media sites for readers will help the progress of independent publishing. To submit a review, go to the book page on any of the sites and follow the links for reviews. Books from independent presses rely on reader to reader communications.

For more information or to order any of our books, visit http://www.fomitepress.com/FOMITE/Our_Books.html

### More Titles from Fomite...

**Novels**
Joshua Amses — *During This, Our Nadir*
Joshua Amses — *Raven or Crow*
Joshua Amses — *The Moment Before an Injury*
Jaysinh Birjepatel — *The Good Muslim of Jackson Heights*
Jaysinh Birjepatel — *Nothing Beside Remains*
David Brizer — *Victor Rand*
Paula Closson Buck — *Summer on the Cold War Planet*
Marc Estrin — *Hyde*
Marc Estrin — *Speckled Vanitie*
Zdravka Evtimova — *Sinfonia Bulgarica*
Daniel Forbes — *Derail This Train Wreck*
Greg Guma — *Dons of Time*
Richard Hawley — *The Three Lives of Jonathan Force*
Lamar Herrin — *Father Figure*
Ron Jacobs — *All the Sinners Saints*
Ron Jacobs — *Short Order Frame Up*
Ron Jacobs — *The Co-conspirator's Tale*
Scott Archer Jones — *A Rising Tide of People Swept Away*

Maggie Kast — *A Free Unsullied Land*
Darrell Kastin — *Shadowboxing with Bukowski*
Coleen Kearon — *Feminist on Fire*
Jan Englis Leary — *Thicker Than Blood*
Diane Lefer — *Confessions of a Carnivore*
Rob Lenihan — *Born Speaking Lies*
Ilan Mochari — *Zinsky the Obscure*
Andy Potok — *My Father's Keeper*
Robert Rosenberg — *Isles of the Blind*
Fred Skolnik — *Rafi's World*
Lynn Sloan — *Principles of Navigation*
L.E. Smith — *The Consequence of Gesture*
L.E. Smith — *Travers' Inferno*
Bob Sommer — *A Great Fullness*
Tom Walker — *A Day in the Life*
Susan V. Weiss — *My God, What Have We Done?*
Peter M. Wheelwright — *As It Is On Earth*
Suzie Wizowaty — *The Return of Jason Green*

## Poetry

Antonello Borra — *Alfabestiario*
Antonello Borra — *AlphaBetaBestiaro*
James Connolly — *Picking Up the Bodies*
Greg Delanty — *Loosestrife*
Mason Drukman — *Drawing on Life*
J. C. Ellefson — *Foreign Tales of Exemplum and Woe*
Anna Faktorovich — *Improvisational Arguments*
Barry Goldensohn — *Snake in the Spine, Wolf in the Heart*
Barry Goldensohn — *The Hundred Yard Dash Man*
Barry Goldensohn — *The Listener Aspires to the Condition of Music*
R. L. Green When — *You Remember Deir Yassin*
Kate Magill — *Roadworthy Creature, Roadworthy Craft*
Tony Magistrale — *Entanglements*
Sherry Olson — *Four-Way Stop*
Janice Miller Potter — *Meanwell*
Joseph D. Reich — *Connecting the Dots to Shangrila*
Joseph D. Reich — *The Hole That Runs Through Utopia*
Joseph D. Reich — *The Housing Market*

Joseph D. Reich — *The Derivation of Cowboys and Indians*
David Schein — *My Murder and Other Local News*
Scott T. Starbuck — *Industrial Oz*
Seth Steinzor — *Among the Lost*
Seth Steinzor — *To Join the Lost*
Susan Thomas — *The Empty Notebook Interrogates Itself*
Sharon Webster — *Everyone Lives Here*
Tony Whedon — *The Tres Riches Heures*
Tony Whedon — *The Falkland Quartet*

## Stories
Jay Boyer — *Flight*
Michael Cocchiarale — *Still Time*
Neil Connelly — *In the Wake of Our Vows*
Catherine Zobal Dent — *Unfinished Stories of Girls*
Zdravka Evtimova — *Carts and Other Stories*
John Michael Flynn — *Off to the Next Wherever*
Elizabeth Genovise — *Where There Are Two or More*
Andrei Guriuanu — *Body of Work*
Derek Furr — *Semitones*
Derek Furr — *Suite for Three Voices*
Zeke Jarvis — *In A Family Way*
Marjorie Maddox — *What She Was Saying*
William Marquess — *Boom-shacka-lacka*
Gary Miller — *Museum of the Americas*
Jennifer Anne Moses — *Visiting Hours*
Martin Ott — *Interrogations*
Jack Pulaski — *Love's Labours*
Charles Rafferty — *Saturday Night at Magellan's*
Kathryn Roberts — *Companion Plants*
Ron Savage — *What We Do For Love*
L.E. Smith — *Views Cost Extra*
Susan Thomas — *Among Angelic Orders*
Tom Walker — *Signed Confessions*
Silas Dent Zobal — *The Inconvenience of the Wings*

## Odd Birds
Micheal Breiner — *the way none of this happened*

Gail Holst-Warhaft — *The Fall of Athens*
Roger Leboitz — *A Guide to the Western Slopes and the Outlying Area*
dug Nap— *Artsy Fartsy*
Delia Bell Robinson — *A Shirtwaist Story*
Peter Schumann — *Planet Kasper, Volumes One and Two*
Peter Schumann — *Bread & Sentences*
Peter Schumann — *Faust 3*

**Plays**
Stephen Goldberg — *Screwed and Other Plays*
Michele Markarian — *Unborn Children of America*

www.ingramcontent.com/pod-product-compliance
Lightning Source LLC
Chambersburg PA
CBHW042233090526
44588CB00001B/6